Dear Everybody,
Admit There's Hurt

Dear Everybody, Admit There's Hurt

Written by Erica N. Wortherly

Illusrated by Daniella & Yanellie Lott

A Note to Adults...

This book is intended to be read with a child or group of children to facilitate a discussion about death and grief. Grief is not only experienced when a loved one dies. It can also be experienced when someone leaves unexpectedly, when a tragedy occurs in the community, or even when major life changes occur such as a move to another city.

Children are resilient. That capacity for resilience is strengthened when trusted adults are able to communicate honestly, openly and empathically with children about difficult transitions that occur as a part of life.

Grief is not something we get over. It is something we get through. Consider the following:
- Acknowledge that death will affect them. Children, like adults, must learn to cope with life's hurts. They learn by observing the behaviors of others.
- To speak honestly with children, you must first acknowledge your own emotional pain.
- Teach children how to deal with rather than repress their feelings of fear, embarrassment, or anger.
- The process of grieving takes time. There is not a specific time frame. Everyone's process is unique to them.
- It is normal to relive experiences, especially during holidays or special occasions.
- Any major change in behavior that lasts longer than a typical mood swing may be a sign to seek additional help outside of the immediate circle of family and friends. Other signs include:
    - Drawings obsessed with death or violence
    - Cruelty to other children or animals
    - Phantom illnesses
    - Obsessive behavior
    - Lethargy or hyperactivity
    - Extreme behaviors inappropriate for the child's age
    - No reaction at all
- Your job is not to prevent grief reactions, but to help meet children's needs during the reactive times to help them recover.

To the children, and the adults who care for them,

who have experienced loss.

You are not alone.

What does a
giraffe have to
do with me losing
somebody close to me? This is really hard.
Oh, not giraffe? Please tell me.

Giraffe? You mean grief.

Grief is an emotion everyone feels when someone leaves or dies. It is a feeling of sadness. Sometimes people cry. Sometimes people are angry. Sometimes people want to be alone. Sometimes people want to be with others who help them understand what happened.

now there's a missing
piece i know they can
rest in peace, but what
about me?
this is grief.

You will hear people say "Sorry for your loss." This person is not lost and you did not lose them. Your life will change. They are no longer here. How does that make you feel? Death may be hard to talk about, but it is a part of life.

Holding my hand again.
Making me laugh again.
They are too far away.
I'm trying to imagine them.

You will miss everything about them: their love, their smile, their help, their hugs, the sound of their voice. Talk with someone and share what you miss the most. Think about what it would be like if they were still with you cheering you on as you continue to grow.

If I got the chance to see
What my loved one could see
My tears might get in the way.
This is too much for me.

It can be hard to believe that someone you love is gone. You may feel angry. One day you might feel fine and one day you will just want to cry. Your feelings will change from day to day. In time, the tears and pain will end. No one will be able to tell you when. For everyone this is different.

Will you keep loving me?
This is hard to believe.
Sometimes, I have scary dreams.
Please, help me keep my memories.

There will be someone who will listen when you need to talk; who will be there when you need to let the pain show. All emotions have energy. Grief may wake you up from your sleep. You might feel scared or alone even when other people are there. Keep a picture, an item that belonged to your loved one, or something to remind you of who they are.

Like a giraffe
that can reach the trees
Grief stretches over all kinds of feelings.
As I grow, I learn and see
Being without them is my new reality.

It's okay to cry. Tears let you know
that you have feelings. Tears are
a release of energy. Tears do not
always mean you are sad or lonely.
Many people cry when they are
happy and excited. It really is okay
to cry. That is how you know you
are alive.

You are human after all.

All humans have emotions.

All emotions work together

and help you know who you are.

You are strong and special.

Grief will not last forever.

Tears and laughter go hand in hand

to help you express all the feelings you can.

*G*rateful-Life is precious. You are here. Look around and notice all of the things to love and appreciate.

*R*hythm-Routines may have been interrupted. As time goes on, a new rhythm may be found while the memories of your loved one will remain.

*I*magination-The mind is always active. It is normal to feel a connection after a loss.

*E*mpathy-You are not alone. Others can understand and share your feelings.

*F*orgiveness-The reasons people die may not be forgotten. But, one of the ways people heal is to allow the joys of life to be bigger than guilt, blame and/or shame.

Dear Everybody, Admit There's Hurt

What does a giraffe have to do with me
Losing somebody close to me?
This is really hard.
Oh, not giraffe? Please tell me.

Now there's a missing piece
I know they can rest in peace
But what about me?
This is grief.

Holding my hand again.
Making me laugh again.
They are too far away.
I'm trying to imagine them.

If I got the chance to see
What my loved one could see
My tears might get in the way.
This is too much for me.

Keep loving me.
This is hard to believe.
Sometimes I have scary dreams.
Please, help me keep my memories.

Like a giraffe that can reach the trees
Grief stretches over all kinds of feelings.
As I grow, I learn and see
Being without them is my new reality.

Grief Recovery Skills & Activities

- Expression
- Creativity
- Physical Activity
- Goal Setting

All your feelings are natural; it is what you do when you are feeling that way that makes the difference.

Expression

Benefits

There are many forms of expression to communicate emotions. You are an individual, and like all situations, you will not respond the same as others. Your personality and process should be respected and nurtured. Some children will readily talk because it frees them. Other children will use constructive energy by staying busy in loving memory of the one who died. Some children are listeners and observe, but don't talk. Still others will process deep within.

Tips
- Talk with a trusted adult.
- Ask questions.
- Discuss memories.
- Look at photos.
- Create a new daily routine.
- Write in a journal.
- Write out memories.
- Write a letter.

Creativity

Benefits

Using creativity is a great way to express emotion. A child (or adult) may discover a new talent or a new passion. It could be something done in the memory of a loved one. Talents can be used to process grief. Imagination and creativity are endless!

Tips

- Create abstract art, paint or draw something to show feelings.
- Write a poem, story, or let the words free flow on a paper or in a journal.
- Sing.
- Write a song.
- Play or learn to play an instrument.

Physical Activity

Benefits

Movement can help you use your energy. When you are feeling difficult emotions, you can have bursts of energy running through your body. Sometimes you will not want to move at all. Moving can help change your mood and help you to feel better.

Tips

- Go for a walk or run.
- Play.
- Swing.
- Join an athletic team.
- Squeeze something, a pillow or stress ball.
- Make up a game.

Goal Setting

Benefits

Focusing on your future can help you to move forward. Think about what you want to do tomorrow, next week, or when you grow up. Think about something you want to learn or try.

Tips

- Write or draw pictures to show what you want to be when you grow up.
- Make a scrap book or collage of pictures to show what you want your future to look like.
- Share your ideas with an adult who can help you.
- Try new activities like learning an instrument or art skills.
- Write your own story.

As I grow,
I learn and see

Being without them
is my new reality.

Erica N. Wortherly specializes in working with educators and parents to improve their understanding of mental health. She travels for speaking engagements in schools, churches and conferences for professional development and caregiver workshops on topics including: self-care practices, mental health awareness, personality differences, and more.

As a former teacher and social worker, she will always be an educator. Erica advocates for shifting mindsets to create more flexible, empathetic and comfortable environments for children and the adults who care for them to thrive.

For more information about Erica N. Wortherly or to order more copies of
Dear Everybody, Admit There's Hurt and other books, please visit www.ericanwortherly.com.

~ ~ ~

Daniella and Yanelie Lott are twin sisters who are high school students majoring in Visual Arts at Douglas Anderson School of the Arts in Jacksonville, FL. Daniella's major is sculpture. She loves to see the outcome of shaping and molding a lump of clay into a work of art. Yanelie's major is painting. She is able to capture the most minute details and her images come to life with the stroke of her paint brush. At any given time, you may see either one of them with their head down, pencil in hand, sketching away and seemingly effortlessly producing reflections of what they see or imagine on the pages of their sketchbooks. Follow them at Facebook.com/AwesomeX2VisualArts/